Diary of a Country Year

THOREAU REVISITED

Judy Manna

THOREAU
REVISITED...

Diary of a Country Year

By Stephen J. Krasemann
And the Editors of Outdoor World

Photographs by the Author except where noted

Outdoor World
Waukesha, Wisconsin

Larger type throughout book by Henry David Thoreau

COUNTRY BEAUTIFUL: *Publisher and Editorial Director:* Michael P. Dineen; *Executive Editor:* Robert L. Polley; *Senior Editors:* Kenneth L. Schmitz, James H. Robb, Steward L. Udall; *Art Director:* Buford Nixon; *Managing Editor:* John M. Nuhn; *Associate Editors:* D'Arlyn M. Marks, Kay Kundinger; *Assistant Editor:* Nancy Backes; *Production Manager:* Donna Griesemer; *Administration:* Brett E. Gries, Bruce L. Schneider; *Administrative Secretary:* Kathleen M. Stoner.

Country Beautiful Corporation is a wholly owned subsidiary of Flick-Reedy Corporation: *President:* Frank Flick; *Vice President and General Manager:* Michael P. Dineen; *Treasurer and Secretary:* August Caamano.

Page 2-3: The green leaves and plumes of a hickory tree announce that spring has hit its stride. *Page 4:* A New England country road invites strollers in blazing autumn. *Page 6-7:* Winter stands poised, ready to strike, after the trees bare their leaves.

Contents

Prologue

My Journal is that of me which would else spill over and run to waste, gleanings from the field which in action I reap. I must not live for it, but in it for the gods. They are my correspondent, to whom daily I send off this sheet postpaid. I am clerk in their counting-room, and at evening transfer the account from day-book to ledger. It is as a leaf which hangs over my head in the path. I bend the twig and write my prayers on it; then letting it go, the bough springs up and shows the scrawl to

heaven. As if it were not kept shut in my desk, but were as public a leaf as any in nature. It is papyrus by the riverside; it is vellum in the pastures; it is parchment on the hills. I find it everywhere as free as the leaves which troop along the lanes in autumn. The crow, the goose, the eagle carry my quill, and the wind blows the leaves as far as I go. Or, if my imagination does not soar, but gropes in slime and mud, then I write with a reed.

THOREAU'S JOURNAL

*I bend the twig and write my prayers on it;
then letting it go, the bough springs up and
shows the scrawl to heaven. . . . The crow,
the goose, the eagle carry my quill, and
the wind blows the leaves as far as I go.*

*A whorled milkweed pod opens its silky fingers to the sun
and awaits a breeze to blow it to other fertile grounds.*

Spring

This is the first really spring day. . . . Something analogous
to the thawing of the ice seems to have taken place in the air.
At the end of winter there is a season in which we are daily
expecting spring, and finally a day when it arrives. . . .

Purple primrose blossoms accent the maze of
new greens along a small, fast-flowing creek.

David Sumner

The doctrines of despair, or spiritual or political tyranny or servitude, were never taught by such as shared the serenity of nature . . . .

Spring rain nurtures a floor of trilliums growing as far as the eye can see.

Olive Glasgow

4 March

This morning two large flocks of Canada geese, in excess of one hundred birds each, flew overhead in a northward direction. Nothing else is giving any sign of spring—neither plants, animals, birds nor consistent warmer weather. Do the geese perchance know something about spring that we do not? After all, they can not just turn around after committing themselves to a two-hundred-mile journey.

Though it is still winter, the geese know that spring is coming; they follow the route of thawing snow and ice northward to the Arctic tundra.

How indispensable our one or two flocks of geese in spring and autumn! . . . Coming to unlock the fetters of northern rivers. Those annual steamers of the air.

14 March

This second week of March brought several occurrences. Two each of killdeer and meadowlark were sighted, and also myriad blackbirds. Snow is still on the ground in the woods and on the northern sides of hills where the sun doesn't reach, and temperatures do not always make it above freezing. But who is better to judge, the birds or we?

26 March

Three inches of snow fell today, but it melted by afternoon.

A red-winged blackbird returns to perch atop cattails, signaling the arrival of the new season.

Olive Glasgow

A jack-in-the-pulpit (opposite) unsheathes with early spring energy. Rainwater collects in the bases of young trilliums (below) growing through the spongy mat of last year's brown leaves.

*Objects are concealed from our view, not
so much because they are out of the course
of visual ray as because we do not bring
our minds and eyes to bear on them.*

5 April

Everything is wet. The woods, the fields, the marshes—all
are saturated with water. On the northern sides of hills traces
of snow remain atop the brown matted leaves.

Everything is also very much alive. Red-winged blackbirds
fly, meadowlarks sing and redtailed hawks tend their eggs.
Burrows are being re-excavated for old and new inhabitants.
Chorus frogs chirp in the swamp; rabbits are on the hillside
chasing each other in trains of up to six in number.

Trees are starting their new growth, but many old trees did
not survive the winter and stand as skeletons until the
decomposition process slowly topples them back to the soil.

But winter reminds us not to build too much hope for
spring by the cool wind that interrupts the warm, windless
moments. This is the season for survival of the fittest. For
snow, freezing temperatures and large amounts of rainfall
may spell doom for the weak and young plants and animals.

11 April

The sun is shining in a blue sky with just a touch of frost
in the air, and at the top of a yet leafless hickory tree a male
red-winged blackbird raises his head, fans his tail and spreads
his wings a bit as he sets forth his fluid song again and again.

24

The warming sun urges these hepaticas to point their broadening leaves toward its light.

Everything is very much alive: Newborn red-tailed hawks (left) show off their fast-growing feathers; two young woodpeckers look out of their treehole nest (below).

R. E. Wood

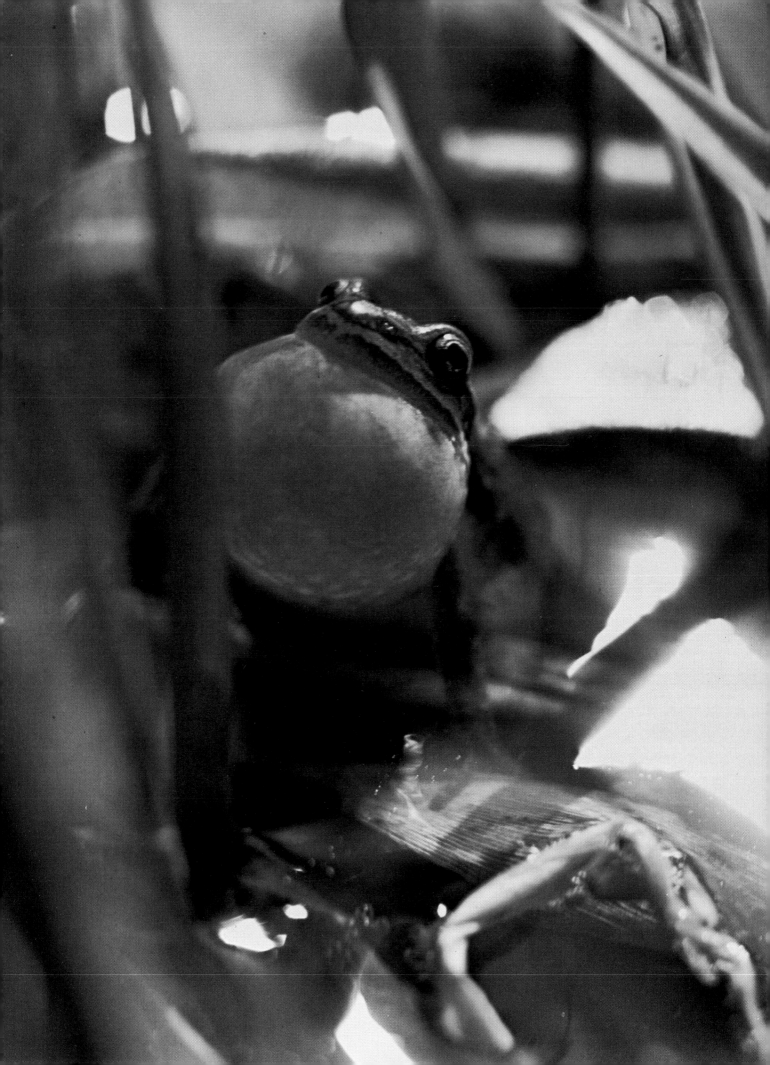

*Listening to hear the earliest wood frogs croaking. I think . . .
it is a singular sound for awakening Nature to make. . . .*

15 April

People consider many things as harbingers of spring. Geese noisily honking as they wing north, robins searching for worms on front yards, purple hepaticas blooming among last year's dead leaves. All can be, and are, signs of spring. But to me the true harbinger of spring is the chorus frog.

All the ice must withdraw from the pond, and the worst cold must be over before the frogs will emerge from the pond bottom.

One night, as quiet blankets the countryside and noises carry like gunshots, the first call comes from the pond. You listen hard; again you hear it, a *crreek* rising in pitch. It sounds like a person running his finger over the teeth of a pocket comb, rubbing the small teeth last.

Our pond is approximately one-half mile from our house, but you can hear the sound loud and clear. Its source is the Western chorus frog—a three-quarter to one-and-a-half-inch-long peepster.

As warm rains move north, the breeding starts in our temporary pond. The male has a vocal pouch which he fills with air and rapidly lets out, producing his croak. The female responds by hopping to the male for breeding.

Eggs are laid and the frogs leave. The tadpoles develop rapidly and leave the pond before it begins to dry up with the arrival of summer heat.

Once in a while, even into the fall, I will be walking near a pond not yet dried up and a *crreek* will resound through the woods. The harbinger of spring, echoing still.

*A male Western chorus frog fills his vocal
pouch with air to produce a loud croak.*

One would think it a novel sight for inland meadows.
Where the cranberry and andromeda and swamp white oak
and maple grow, here is a mimic sea, with its gulls.

16 April

On my return from the pond today, I chanced to sight a splotch of purple in my path. I thought, it couldn't be flowers. I hadn't found any plant growth that far progressed to bloom. But there it was — two clumps of blossoming hepaticas sheltered by fallen logs and warm leaves, supreme growing conditions. It does the mind good to know that a true herald of spring has finally arrived.

The delicately tinted blossoms of hepaticas rising
on thin, hairy stems are true heralds of spring.

There is just as much beauty visible to us in the landscape as we are prepared to appreciate, — not a grain more . . . .

25 April

The day dawns with silver droplets falling ever so fresh from the gray skies.

The marsh, already saturated to the brim, is bristling with life. Red-winged blackbird females arrived last week and the males are constantly fighting among themselves whenever a female chances to venture near. Kingfisher males are bickering over a choice female, while the swallows and martins skim the water's surface, searching for insects, appearing oblivious to the mating urge.

Raccoon tracks dot the paths from the marsh to the woods, killdeer roam the edges of the marsh searching for food, woodcocks tumble from the sky, and a thirteen-lined ground squirrel sits upright wondering what to do about my intrusion.

Once in the woods a quick census reveals blackberry bushes covering their thorns with leaves, columbine growing like miniature towers, shooting-stars starting to send out their flower stalks, and hepaticas blooming.

It is time to keep your eyes open; if you blink twice the now will be gone, with all its drapings, until next year.

The abundant life at the marsh includes a pair of belted kingfishers; their loud, rattling calls can be heard across the water.

The fragile beauty of small blossoms brighten the forest floor (below). The tips of the wild columbine (opposite) are storehouses for rich nectar, gathered by hummingbirds.

Marsh marigolds (right) thrust their gilded blossoms above the rich soil of the marsh. A stump will decay and provide valuable nutrients to future growth (below).

Olive Glasgow

Within a little more than a fortnight the woods,
from bare twigs, have become a sea of verdure. . . .

Thomas H. Algire

Maple and white pine branches vie to reach the sun (opposite). Still wearing the color of their buds, oak leaves (above) are one of the last to turn green.

The dandelions' parachute seeds will be blown by the wind to other places to take hold in new soil.

9 May

Spring arrives to stay with consistent warm, moist days. The first plants to be noticed with the change are the grasses. Gradually the drab brown landscape transforms to a rich green, and spring grows. But as grasses grow, so do other plants and before long all you notice are the flashy trilliums, shooting-stars, hepaticas and dandelions. It is during this time that grass goes through the most beautiful stage of its growth cycle. The flowers that emerge from its glumes are as fascinating or stunning as any other flower of woods or field.

No petals exist on this floret; it consists of three stamens and a single ovary surmounted by two feathery stigmas. Watch the grass, look for the yellow or red bells to hang from the spikelets. It will be one flower you will notice every year.

12 May

With the weather being consistently warm and with sufficient moisture in the ground for growth, the rivers have ceased their swelling. Marsh marigolds bloom in the puddles left by the receding water.

Dandelions are going to seed, sending their diminutive parachutes bobbing through the air.

It would be a long list to name all the wildflowers, animals and insects that are starting growth. Instead one might say every plant, insect and animal is growing.

Nature's watch is truly on time.

A field of dandelions (above) was meant for wandering through and reveling in nature's changes. Mayapple leaves form a forest pattern (opposite).

Nature never makes haste; her systems revolve at an even pace. The buds swell imperceptibly, without hurry or confusion, as though the short spring days were an eternity.

The new growths of a red pine branch will mature
by summer's end and lose their light green color.

17 May

The woods are shrouded in green — no mosquitoes yet. Morels are out after yesterday's rain.

Rain falls frequently. It waters nature's gardens, freshens the air and washes the nests of birds, eliminating scents that would build quickly if left to accumulate.

Every spring is different. Some bring snow or drenching rains, some bring hot weather and drought, and then there is this spring with just the right temperatures and amount of rainfall. It is just as you would picture spring after a winter of hoping and anticipating.

20 May

The woods have changed; in a couple of days, they have become mystical forests. The pale-green of early spring has turned, suddenly, to a rich dark-green of summer, even though the leaves are not yet fully grown. The grass, now knee-high, is overtowered by the mayapples ready to open their single blossoms to the insects of the woods. The wood geranium is the newest plant arrival. Trillium is pinking at the edges and will soon die, sending its petals falling like soft clouds to decompose in the never-ending cycle of the seasons.

Strange that so few ever come to the woods to see how the pine lives and grows and spires, lifting its evergreen arms to the light, — to see its perfect success. . . .

Summer

Each phase of nature, while not invisible, is yet not too distinct and obtrusive. It is there to be found when we look for it, but not demanding our attention.

Colorful fireweed flames across clearings and meadows as summer reaches its fulfillment.

*At length the summer's
eternity is ushered in . . . .*

*The deep, rich shades of summer are
evident along the shore of a lake.*

50

28 May

Officially summer does not arrive until June 21, but I think it has arrived already. Mosquitoes hail summer, and the martins hail mosquitoes; both are present in good numbers.

All the fragile spring flowers — hepatica, spring anemone, trillium — are gone, and the stronger, deeper-colored flowers — wild rose, columbine, wood geranium — are dominating the forest floor.

Shooting-stars hide in the shade of the woods, a few crickets are creaking out a harmony known to everyone who lies sleepless on hot summer nights, and the early babies are out and about. Robins are full grown; the only way to tell them from the adults is to look for the stripes still evident on their breasts. Baby bunnies nibble succulent grasses by the roadside, still ignorant to the rolling death of automobiles, often running and darting in front of cars. But I guess they never learn because rabbits are easily the most car-killed animal in our area.

The hot air is also starting to come alive. Small insects glisten in the setting sun, wings shimmering, seconds before they become splotches on the auto windshield.

Spring showers are giving way to the clear, dew-laden mornings of summer, with the afternoons hot and humid.

Wild roses are now dominating some of the forest floor — the spring flowers are gone.

Vic McLeran

*A young cottontail feeds on the roadside's grasses (above).
Dawn throws its light on dew, a milkweed plant and a spider's
runner web (opposite, top). Snapping turtles (opposite,
bottom) prey on fish eggs, ducklings and goslings.*

R. Greenler

. . . I see two and perhaps three young striped squirrels . . .
They are running about, yet rather feebly, nibbling the
grass, etc., or sitting upright, looking very cunning.

Until this year thirteen-lined ground squirrels have remained in the surrounding fields, but this spring a pair entered the mowed portion of our lawn.

They tunneled escape routes under a hundred square feet of our yard. At this point our human neighbors would do one of three things: poison them, flood them out or shoot them. We accepted another alternative — let them stay unmolested.

Our pair was apparently mated; they gave our yard two young babies. All summer their training was in earnest. They learned how to "freeze" with every unknown shadow. A bluejay's warning sent them scurrying to their burrow entrance. Food knowledge, what to eat and not, was learned. Soon the heat came and they disappeared — estivation.

With the summer waning they came forth once more to gather as many nuts as possible before the falling leaves and temperature forced them into the opposite of estivation — hibernation.

5 June

Our young thirteen-lined ground squirrels are starting to show their faces. Often they become confused upon seeing a car approaching and they will run directly ahead of the moving car instead of going to the safety of their den. If they do not learn rapidly, a hawk, cat or weasel may take advantage of their youthful ignorance.

Creatures of summer: Wilson's snipe (top) is
a common marsh bird; the attractive thirteen-
lined ground squirrel (bottom) is a true burrower and
digs many tunnels leading to its underground home.   Overleaf: *Seeding dandelions cover the fields.*

There was a time when the beauty and the music were all within, and I sat and listened to my thoughts, and there was a song in them.

6 June

Seeding dandelions cover patches of fields, making them look like cotton fields in bloom. And tonight the goatsbeard, that huge dandelion, was trying hard to soak up enough sun and warmth to open its flowers for the business of local insects.

With clear skies during the day, the number of red sunsets is increasing.

It is futile to try to observe everything that is happening from day to day. It is happening too fast, and besides, it is happening with different actors on each stage — woods, fields, swamps, ponds and rivers. But just to fill your eyes with the new sights spurs you to grasp as much as possible from each changing day before it is gone.

Silhouetted by a yellow sun, the details of a species of tall grass are starkly apparent.

12 June

Every time a person thinks about something he is in a different mood; he is feeling life in the one way he can — through his emotions.

Summer days are a great time for emotions of life. It may start with the wonderment of a dew drop on a blade of quack grass, before the sun evaporates the droplet into moisture for clouds. And it may end with an orange sunset, tinklings of frost building on that same blade of quack grass.

To become invincible a person must first lose all his emotions, for emotions are the very thing that would lead to his downfall. I would not want to lose my emotions, for emotions are life being felt.

18 June

Red-tailed hawk and great-horned owl young are making mock lift-offs from their lofty nests in preparation for their first flights in a few weeks. The first flight must not fail; if it would, it could mean doom in the form of crippling or death by predators.

Life is passing us by as fast as grass is growing. Insects, birds and mammals show us in one year what our lives take eighty years to complete. All the pitfalls and joys are condensed into a few months of living.

Summer is the wonder of morning dew drops glistening on bent blades of grass.

*The wind that blows
Is all that any-
body knows.*

22 June

It is intriguing the way nature works. When the mother kingfisher starts to bring minnows to her babies, they are small. But as the young grow, so does the size of the minnows, so the parents need not catch any more minnows per day to satisfy their offspring's hunger.

24 June

Once again the lazy days of summer are here with their time of plenty.

Dawn mists from the cool night lie on the fields, casting a haze on the early morning sun.

Olive Glasgow

Woodchucks (above) like to sun themselves on rocks and fallen trees.
A white-tailed doe (opposite) enjoys the cool waters of a stream.

Olive Glasgow

The green berries of the bittersweet nightshade (above)
turn to orange and then red. A rose-breasted grosbeak
contrasts with the greens of summer (below).

It is necessary to sacrifice the greater value to the less.
I would rather never taste chicken's meat or hen's eggs than
never to see a hawk sailing through the upper air again.

28 June

Wild barley is letting its hair blow freely in the wind, and the bittersweet nightshade is starting to form green berries from its purple flowers. In time the berries will turn yellow to orange and then to red.

Blue, green and brown damselflies have filled the area surrounding the marsh.

Did you ever think what would happen to a sick wild animal, even if it was sick for only three days? It would almost surely die, either of starvation or at the claws of a predator. So when you think of animals living for even five years, that means they could not have ever been sick, and that is quite a record under their conditions.

30 June

A yearling red-tail hawk was causing quite a stir in the corner of the woods, and I do not think he quite knew why. A single hairy woodpecker started the ruckus, and his complaining brought the usual gripers, the bluejays. Quickly following was a Baltimore oriole, a male red-winged blackbird and two robins wondering what the cause for confusion was.

A squirrel came halfway down a tree but showed little concern, and all this while a male rose-breasted grosbeak drifted from bush to bush, never uttering a peep of protest, just content to witness the whole event.

Shortly the hawk drifted up into the sky, harassed all the way by blackbirds, and floated to a different, calmer area of his world.

1 July

A spider, its web still moist and heavy with morning dew, has a careless grasshopper that hopped in the wrong direction when a bird's shadow covered him a second too long. At the moment the grasshopper struck the web the spider was already sensing its prey by means of a silken strand held in its foreleg for just such a purpose.

Descending rapidly to the kicking grasshopper, the spider instinctively knew what to do. The grasshopper was turned round and round, slowly becoming cocooned in an abundance of viscid fluid which hardens into silk. Sometime during the wrapping the spider bit the grasshopper so that it would die quickly. Now with a meal secured, the spider meticulously went about rebuilding its web for its next victim.

3 July

The marsh is brimming with water from a week-long rain. A walk along the marsh perimeter flushes many water birds, and there certainly are enough different varieties of dragonflies and damselflies buzzing and flitting around the river's edge. There are some blue bodies and pure black wings, some brown bodies and transparent wings, and some blue bodies with wings half black and half clear, a splotch of black on the clear wingtips.

Their protuberant eyes swivel, picking up any movement — danger, prey or the continual motions made by the wind. An extremely agile insect, the dragonfly is almost impossible to catch with a butterfly net.

A spider web, heavy with morning dew, can capture any insect which travels too close.

70

All this was accomplished in an instant by a kind of fire out of the heavens called lightning, or a thunderbolt, accompanied by a crashing sound. For what purpose? . . . If we trust our natural impressions, it is a manifestation of brutish force or vengeance, more or less tempered with justice.

6 July

Storms build and the rain never comes. And then suddenly one materializes with all the fury of rain, wind, cool temperatures and tornado watches. Such a storm is blowing tonight. Lightning fills the sky and for a fraction of a second, daylight returns. This is quickly followed by a house-shaking blast of thunder that crashes for ten seconds without letup. Lightning bolts and thunder often fill the nights with a feeling of power. With lightning having up to a million volts of electricity, it is no wonder man worshiped such things as the sun and lightning.

Tornado warnings, thunderstorms and high winds are common to this season. Animals know when the storms are coming, perhaps by a built-in barometer. Ants cover entrances, chipmunks hole up, and birds hurriedly stuff their young with food. Once the rain starts, the woods and fields stand still.

Rain does so much for the landscape's appearance and sound. Plants start to grow almost visibly, and the birds are so happy, taking baths in the fresh puddles, that the air is saturated with song.

Lightning bolts fill the night with a feeling of power (top), but the accompanying rain does much to clean and freshen the land (bottom).

Olive Glasgow

21 July

Turtles are laying their eggs by the edges of lakes and streams. It may be ten weeks before they hatch. Upon hatching each turtle will have a yellowish yolk-sac attached to it for the first twenty-four to thirty-six hours. The young will live on this, and not until this membrane is dissolved does the turtle's shell begin to harden. It will be about one year before it achieves its bone hardness.

A turtle ventures from the water to lay as many as three hundred eggs in the sand.

I am affected by the thought that the earth nurses these eggs. . . . Though the immediate mother turtle abandons her offspring, the earth and sun are kind to them. . . . Thus the earth is the mother of all creatures.

22 July

The most sickening sight of these days are the bodies of youngsters dead on the roadsides. A baby, new to the world, starting life for the first year, is suddenly faced with the headlights of a speeding killer — a killer so fast that even the quickened reflexes of a wild animal are not sufficient to avoid death.

The killer is the automobile and the victims are baby animals, particularly baby skunks and raccoons. Their bodies lie lifeless in the road with maggots and carrion beetles eating them to pieces.

It is very sad that the automobile is so excellent a killer.

The raccoon preys on small marsh life, but is itself prey to many other animals.

Olive Glasgow

24 July

A dawn walk starts with the cool air and the moon shining brightly in the sky. But by the time you have discovered a caterpillar, newly emerged from its chrysalis, eating dew-covered raspberries, the world has changed. The once-shining moon is now pale against the bright blue sky. Ants that were covered with cold dew are now making their way toward the aphids they farm during the daylight hours.

Indian pipe lifts palely, almost unseen in the dark reaches of the woods, its translucent hook bowing silently, matching all that is in the quiet dawn.

25 July

This morning I saw what must have been the work of a thousand spiders. A whole field was laced with webs and lines of silk leading to the webs. There must have been two hundred webs, all laden with dew, and not an inhabitant in sight. I do not know if the webs were there all this time.

The tiny Indian pipe fungus bows silently, almost unseen in the dark reaches of the woods.

Olive Glasgow

*Observed the spiders at work. . . . I see some of . . .
their fine lines though it requires a very favorable
light to detect them, they are so fine. . . .*

A small forest road is dappled in shadow
(below). A field laced with spider webs
(right) opens the eyes to new wonders.

26 July

A few hot days, a few cool days: it is late summer already. Red and black raspberries are ripening on the roadsides. Some mornings are cooled with heavy dews making the eyes squint to look toward the brilliant sparkles that ornament the plants. Seed pods are forming on the milkweed; cicadas whirr-saw during the day, and at night crickets chirp. The swallows have young sitting on electric wires watching their parents catching insects; kingfishers are scarcely watching their offspring as they are quite proficient at catching minnows and require little supplementary feeding from mom and dad. And the immature red-tailed hawks are as able at flying as their parents; the only visible difference are the black bands on their otherwise crimson tails.

29 July

Question mark butterflies have been hatching for the last week, splitting the small plasticine case that has protected them from the elements for the last three weeks.

Ragweed is forming the small blossoms that will become the "death bombs" of many people. Microscopic capsules will release billions of pollen to irritate the nostrils and lungs of humans with the affliction called hay fever.

A question mark butterfly emerges from its chrysalis, which has protected it for three weeks.

R. Greenler

The green frog (above) lives up to ten years, longer than most other frogs. The dagger moth caterpillar (opposite) must constantly eat vegetation.

R. Greenler

I find my clothes covered with
young caterpillars these days.

1 August

CATERPILLARS: fuzzy ones, smooth ones, drab ones, colored ones, striped ones, checked ones, small ones, large ones, soft ones, sharp ones. From spring until fall, thousands go through hundreds of metamorphoses.

Many do not make it through the complete cycle. From the day a caterpillar emerges into the atmosphere it is in continual peril. Predators are a main danger: An assassin bug can find a caterpillar in its helpless upside-down position, pending a change to a chrysalis, and kill it immediately. All that remains is a dried hollow skin after the assassin bug finishes sucking all the nourishing juices from the caterpillar. The elements are also deadly: A premature freeze, a flooding rain or a grass fire could kill the caterpillars.

But many do make it. Constantly eating and shedding too-small skins, they progress from egg to larva to chrysalis, and finally emerge a butterfly. All in one summer.

Nature's small world: A striped monarch caterpillar crawls along a milkweed branch (top); a robber fly lands on a yarrow blossom (bottom).

. . . The pods or follicles of the Asclepias Syriaca now point upward. . . . They are already bursting. I release some seeds with the long, fine silk attached. The fine threads fly apart at once. . . .

10 August

I have found six different varieties of the nine milkweeds believed to be in our area: common, purple, swamp, four-leaved, poke and whorled. Of these six, I am partial to one — the whorled milkweed.

It is the smallest of the family, only one to two feet tall with many whorled-linear leaves. It prefers dry slopes and gravelly soil.

A patch of whorled milkweed is one of the best places to be on a warm summer day; it abounds with insect life. Small ambush bugs await prey in some blossoms; spiders weave webs to snare low-flying insects, and butterflies and bees flit from flower to flower pollinating.

Fertilized flowers change to seed pods, and with fall they burst, sending seeds to fly with each whim of the wind. At dusk the sun illuminates every hair on each seed's parachute, producing miniature suns everywhere one looks. With closer inspection you can catch all the colors of the spectrum in each hair.

A patch of whorled milkweed, laden with dew, catches the glint of the early morning sun.

Who would believe in prophecies . . . that the world would end this summer, while one milkweed with faith matured its seeds?

*The flowers of summer: Fireweed
blossoms (below) brighten the edge
of a spruce forest; coneflowers (right)
lift themselves high into the air.*

16 August

Hay fever has started today. The invisible pollen grains are sifting their way through the respiratory systems of humans, causing sneezing, itching and watering eyes, along with constant nose blowing. Hay fever is not fatal, but at times it makes the afflicted wish it was.

17 August

The ambush bug waits rock-still, coloration closely matching the milkweed blossom upon which it hunts. Softly a painted lady butterfly lands to sip nectar. Too fast for the eye to see, small mantislike legs strike the butterfly's head and grasp tight as a steel trap. Following quickly, a sharp beak pierces the captured body and the ambush bug begins to feast. Having sucked the juices from the butterfly's body, it releases its hold and the butterfly drops to the ground. Many other cycles now begin to work, and the painted lady decays, the valuable nutrients that are left going back into the soil from whence they came. The ambush bug, too, now filled with other nutrients, will eventually be eaten by another predator or decay into the soil.

Late summer means suffering for some, for the air will soon be filled with pollen from the common ragweed.

*All the earth is dripping wet. I am
surprised to feel how warm the water is. . . .*

The cooling rain wets maidenhair ferns (opposite). Raindrops, each refracting the images of the world about them, gather at the tips of spruce needles (above).

*A male black-winged damselfly lands briefly on a leaf (above).
The great spangled fritillary butterfly (opposite) catches the
early sun's warmth from a perch of red pine needles.*

22 August

The world constantly changes, but different characters performing makes it enjoyable instead of monotonous.

Plants are plants; the same ones grow year after year. Milkweed seeds blew in the wind last year; burdock bloomed its purple flowers last year, and toadflax (butter and eggs) also flowered last year. But again each year it is new. You watch the flowers develop; you anticipate the landscape changing colors from white to yellow and in the fall, to red. It is like revisiting with friends.

26 August

Fall has whispered of its coming days. The mornings are almost cold, humidity has lessened and the raindrops chill instead of warm the body.

Mosquitoes are diminishing, much to the relief of suffering mammals.

Another good sign are the birds flying overhead, showing gaps in the wings where primary feathers once existed.

It is time for man to prepare for the winter. It is still months away, but there is canning and building repairs to attend.

The changing world: Fleabane blossoms whiten the summer greenery (top); a trout lily spreads its six-pointed bloom between its leaves (bottom).

Nature's artistry can be seen in the pattern of a branch of hophornbeam leaves.

*How much beauty in decay! . . . Yet, perchance,
to the vegetable kingdom such a revelation of ribs is
as repulsive as the skeleton in the animal kingdom.*

28 August

The plants and the trees have ceased to grow, having added all the major growth for the current year.

The forest floor is dying. Plants that once held dew to drench my pants to the knees are withering and falling. One can see great openings on the floor, openings to see once-hidden chipmunks, squirrels and minute mushrooms springing from the decaying debris after each shower.

Leek is exposing black berries in clusters of three, and milkweed plants are yellowing and dropping their leaves.

Death is in abundance, as is life. A monarch caterpillar's skin, dry and hollow, hangs from the spot it picked to change to a chrysalis because another insect discovered a meal that could not flee. Dragonflies snap paper wings in the dusk, devouring any small insect that chances to fly above the grass. Even the bumblebee is secured under a leaf to spend the night.

Yellow coral mushrooms grow from the decaying debris on the forest floor.

A summer sunset (above) brightens the hearts of those who live in the country. A monarch butterfly, newly emerged from its chrysalis (opposite), clings to a stalk of white asters.

2 September

Monarch butterflies, the majority just out of their chrysalis and glowing with orange color, flocked en masse over the goldenrod patches. All were making ready for migration, none showing concern for mating and trying to start another generation this late in the year.

Orb spiders spin their webbed traps all over the fields hoping to snare unsuspecting insects. How is it possible for the orb spider to time its hatch when food is most plentiful, particularly grasshoppers? The temperatures must match the grasshoppers' preference, and through evolution nature is directly caring for the existence of her species by timing the birth of predator and prey to coincide.

An orb spider (top) waits for insects to get caught on its newly woven silk trap, as a nearby lynx spider crawls on a leaf (bottom).

James H. Robinson

The fox seems to get his living by industry and perseverance. . . . He belongs to a noble family.

5 September

The red fox is king of our woods. We don't have wolves, cougars or bears. In fact, there are only three large wild animals in our woods: the deer, the raccoon and the fox.

We are fortunate enough to have a fox den in the back of our woods. Early this March, the vixen gave birth to three kits. The babies did not ask to be fox, and if they knew what prejudices man has against them, I don't think they would understand. But wild animals "accept" their circumstances and live the best life they can.

Hunters kill them on sight, anytime; trappers trap them for their hides, which women relish, and many continue to use poison, a horrible death, and for what?

Everyone says the fox will increase this year because of rabbits being in such great numbers. I hope so, because the fox is an animal few people see and if their numbers increase, their chance for survival will be greatly improved.

To many people the life of one fox means nothing. The death of the whole species would cause a few more to show concern. But what can be done to change man's attitude, to erase his prejudgment, and to let him take each matter and see to it that the opinion he forms is fair? If there is an answer it would change the whole world. Maybe in the future. . . .

The foxes' beautiful red fur makes them one of the handsomest of all forest animals.

*The autumnal tints grow gradually darker
and duller, but not less rich to my eye.*

Autumn

*Sumac brightens the fields early,
giving promise of more color to come.
Overleaf: Then, without warning, the trees
turn red and yellow seemingly overnight.*

*We go admiring the pure and delicate tints of
fungi on the surface of the damp swamp. . . .*

11 September

A few maples are turning odd branches a red color, and
elms are sending yellow to a few leaves, but sumac has them
all beat — it began turning red a week ago.

Small white asters are all over the field; ragweed is letting
up, dropping seeds to the ground, preserving its potency until
next season.

Fall has arrived with its brisk nights and pleasantly cool
days, its brilliant colors, and its promise of winter.

18 September

Fall is the time of maturing in the plant world. Hickories
and oaks have nuts weighing down the ends of the branches.
The berry bushes — blueberries, blackberries, elderberries —
are ripe and juicy, and naturally the birds and animals harvest
the fruits as soon as possible.

Trees, shrubs, grasses, flowers — every blossom previously
fertilized by insects or wind is now loosing a fully developed
seed. Growth has already stopped.

Like its photosynthesizing cousins, other plants have
stopped growing too. These plants have grown unnoticed
underground. Thin, threadlike strands of mycelium have
inched together to form mattbeds that are the mushroom

(continued on page 116)

Fall breeds mushrooms superior in color and variety;
Pholiota destruens *decorates the forest floor.*

114

plants. The mushroom we see is only the fruit of the mushroom plant. While it takes a whole summer of development for other plants to seed, the mushroom fruits and dies within a day or two.

A heavy, saturating rain will certainly bring mushrooms fruiting in a forest, but the fall breeds mushrooms superior in color and variety to any other period of the year. They are truly fall's "flowers."

Probably the most common known member of the mushroom and fungi family is the puffball (*Calvatia gigantea*), a huge, white, globular ball that often reaches diameters of two and one-half feet. (I saw one once that measured four feet, five inches.)

Other mushrooms and fungi are also in abundance. Blazing sulphur shelf (*Lateiporus sulphureus*) hangs from rotting stumps; it is of the pore fungi family and is flaming orange above and brilliant yellow on its lower shelf. The *Flammulina velutipes* or winter mushroom is an orange mushroom with a sticky cap. It is always found growing in clusters on dead, rotting elm and aspen trees.

One other common and noticeable mushroom is *Marasmius*. It goes under the common name of "little wheels," a fitting name because the caps do resemble wheels. This mushroom is only one to three inches in height, but is probably the most abundant mushroom in our woods.

Numerous, fragile-looking winter mushrooms
cluster on the trunk of a dead tree.

The edges of the inky cap mushroom turn black and watery as the spores are released.

22 September

As you walk through the fields you must constantly be on the lookout for tops of grasses bent over, like a strung bow. If you don't take heed, you may knock down a spider's web and walk away with the spider attached to you, only to find him later, a startling discovery, crawling up your neck.

The clouds are looking like the beginning of winter — drifting carpets of gray without any shape or form. A person can almost imagine the first flakes of snow floating from the sky onto his nose, melting and running down it, tickling as they go. But along with the thoughts of snow is the unpleasant reminder of bitter, numbing cold.

26 September

Every chipmunk in the woods is preparing for winter with endless energy, constantly searching for non-perishable food-stuffs to store in underground bins. Any perishable food discovered is eaten on the spot with a quick, nervous nibbling.

Basking on a sun-warmed stump is a luxury of summer past. But if the chipmunk is to enjoy that luxury next year, it must store enough food to last the winter and into the beginning of spring when no food has yet grown.

Chipmunks must store enough food to last
through the winter and the beginning of spring.

27 September

One of the noblest plants in the forest in the jack-in-the-pulpit. In spring, it thrusts a swordlike stalk out of the warm, saturated soil. This soon bursts into two stalks, each bearing three parted leaves. Now standing one and one-half feet tall, a lordly greenish spathe and spadix with many minute, green-yellow flowers comes forth.

Summer changes each fertilized flower into a green berry, and as fall comes the berries first turn orange and then deep crimson. By this time the leaves have withered and died; all that remains is a brilliant red wand standing above the carpet of yellow and brown leaves on the forest floor.

30 September

Red-tailed hawks, in numbers of twenty and thirty, can be seen soaring in circles high in the sky, drifting ever southward out of sight.

With the first freeze just around the corner, some of the Canada geese are starting their trip south. They leave me with a feeling that I am losing a close friend, and I am saddened.

Rain has brought out the best in mushrooms. It is a great time to sample all the various mushroom dishes, with caution because some species are poisonous.

The reds of autumn: Crimson berries of the jack-in-the-pulpit (top) will last until early winter; a scarlet fungus (bottom) grows from the rotting forest floor.

2 October

Woolly bears are everywhere, a migration to compare with the lemmings of the Arctic countries. The brown and black striped caterpillars are moving en masse over the roads.

They must be able to sense the coming cold because a suitable hibernation site is what drives them on. After a summer of feeding, they must now locate a rock mound or a brush pile that will shelter them from the winter elements.

Come spring the winter survivors will spin cocoons and transform themselves into the tawny-colored Isabella moths. These moths in turn will lay the eggs that will eventually grow to be the woolly bears of next fall.

Hibernating woolly bears must search for a brush pile or a rock mound to shelter them from the coming cold.

4 October

Fall color is in the plants. Yellow mayapples dangle from dead stalks, red jack-in-the-pulpit seeds cluster, and purple grapes cling to the fencerows.

Brown is also the color of fall: Queen Anne's lace, its flowers closed in the shape of a bird's nest, curled dock and tall mullen ornament the barren field.

Soon the turtles and frogs will descend to the lower waters and bury themselves in the mud for the long and almost oxygenless winter, breathing ever so slowly through membranes in their skin.

Hordes of blackbirds alight in the dead trees. They resemble animated leaves of yesteryear. Flying to the ground, they systematically comb the grasses for food; I would hate to be an insect trying to save my life.

6 October

Three seasons have come and soon the fourth will arrive. What have we done to save it for our memories? We live but we seldom see, and if we see, it is all too soon forgotten. Memories are what the latter years in life are made of.

*A cluster of common milkweed seeds
offer a different kind of autumn color.*

The berries of false Solomon's seal hang from a fence (above). Shagbark hickory leaves (opposite), once tossed by summer breezes, lie dead, beautiful in their colors.

I listen to the sharp, dry rustle of the withered oak leaves. This is the voice of the wood now.

Color stands for all ripeness and success. We have dreamed that the hero should carry his color aloft, as a symbol of the ripeness of his virtue.

11 October

Color has started in quantity. Burrs stick to socks in numbers to work their way into your skin.

Nuthatches are becoming the voice of the woods; chickadees are noticeable once more, hidden in the woods all summer.

Many leaves are on the ground, and there are snow reports to the north of us. Chipmunks are no longer about in the woods.

Windy days spread milkweed parachutes over the fields. Every plant is dying. Now we await the first snow. Some with reluctance, some with anticipation, and still others with joy. They are the people who feel all the seasons.

15 October

Leaves alone know the secret of a beautiful death.

26 October

Some trees are bare, but many are still fully leaved. The first snow will come any day now, but it probably won't stay. The days sometimes reach fifty degrees, still warm.

If they were human, maples would envy the spruce keeping their needles; but spruce needles do not have a last, glorifying splash of color.

Olive Glasgow

A toad finds a shelf fungus growth perfect for resting (above).
Brown is the color of the woods now — fallen maple leaves
(right) lie dead amid an oak stump and broken branches.

I wandered over bare fields . . . What nutriment can I extract from these bare twigs? Starvation stares me in the face. ''Nay, nay!'' said a nuthatch. . . .

A late autumn sun, already below the horizon, strikes a layer of thin clouds; sunsets seem more glorious this time of year.

Winter

The bleached herbage of the fields is like frost, and frost like snow, and one prepares for the other.

Bent over and buried under a load of snow, marsh grass is protected from the cold winds.

John M. Nuhn

R. Greenler

The first spitting of snow — This consisted almost entirely of pellets. . . . The plowed fields were for a short time whitened with them.

16 November

The first snow fell last week, followed by one week of below-freezing temperatures. Birds are flocking to the feeder.

It's a long four months ahead, and only the birds remain, pieces of life. All the plants are brown skeletons; nothing new grows any more. It is survival time — rest for some, hardships to endure for the remainder.

7 December

The mornings are sometimes frosty with traces of snow falling. Patches of snow rest in the pockets of grass where the sun does not reach. Just winter waiting.

The first snow catches some leaves still on the trees (top). Afterward, a tufted titmouse visits the feeder (bottom). Overleaf: Minute crystals of frost turn still-green grass into icy blades.

Every part of nature teaches that the passing away of one life is the making room for another.

12 December

Plants continue to disperse their pepperlike seeds, which are scattered by the winds. They fall all over the snow, looking like particles of soot. Some go for mouse and bird food, some to rot, and a select few to absorb water and minerals in the spring to continue the species.

The wind chases undulating masses of snowflakes across the surface of the road, back and forth, seemingly going in no particular direction. Some of the snowflakes, blown from the sides of the roads, stop in calms to form huge snowdrifts.

The bee's nest is alive. If you press your ear to the tree hole, you will hear the buzzing of wings constantly circulating the air to warm the hive. It will grow with warmer days if the hive's honey holds out and no predator finds it.

24 December

The northern lights have glowed brightly the last two nights.

Faces of winter: Frost-covered whorled milkweed (opposite, top) continues to disperse its seeds; the honeybees' buzzing warms their nest in the cleft of a tree (opposite, left); of the hundreds of poison ivy seeds in these berries (opposite, right), only some may grow to maturity.

31 December

The remnants of a small painted turtle's shell lays shattered on a roadside, bordered by a foot of snow. I wondered why he hadn't hibernated, and could visualize his last sluggish steps before the cold numbed him so much that he was a sitting target for the car's tires.

A cold night, from twenty-eight degrees in the day to zero at night, creates a fog. Frost is forming and twinkles now in the full moonlight. Snow creaks when walked on.

8 January

Dust snow is falling — snow so light and dry it almost resists gravity. Each step puffs up clouds of snow, which lightly settles back into your footprints, like dust on a dry summer road. Gently, almost begrudgingly, it alights on everything, glittering in the moonlight. This is the freshest snow to fall; it produces quiet and beauty.

The moon glows with a touch of beauty. Silent moving clouds reflect, in order, circles of gossamer, yellow and red around the moon.

Circles of gossamer surround the winter moon (top). The sunlit tops of grass (bottom) have a contrasting effect against the snowy background.

R. Greenler

Judy Sumner

Nature is full of genius, full of the divinity; so that not a snowflake escapes its fashioning hand. . . .

15 January

Winter is at its fullest. The last few days have had below zero temperatures, fifteen below zero one morning.

Today there was real blizzard — high winds and fiercely blowing snow. Outside my windows I could see nothing else moving. Such a storm drives even those creatures most adapted to winter behind some shelter.

After the storm our woods had a new look: Snow had blown onto everything horizontally, leaving the opposite sides untouched.

Thin twigs support the burden of moisture-laden snow (top) as it alights on everything in the woods (bottom) — this is winter at its fullest.

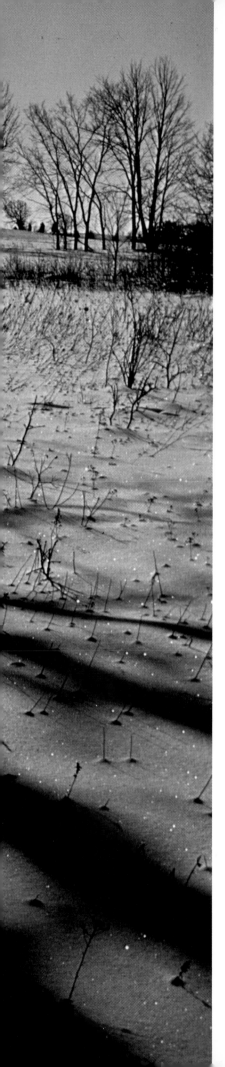

Winter's long shadows (left) are cast over the frozen, covered earth. Prickly-ash and goldenrod plants (above) are only brown skeletons in the snow.

David Parmelee

19 January

Driving home one late winter's night, while watching the snow-packed road so as not to slide into the ditch, I caught a blur of motion as the snow suddenly became animated. The motion took form as a snowy owl sluggishly lifted from the snowscape to boomerang into my headlights' illumination and back into the cold night. When it disappeared, as if it were a fleeting hallucination, I thought of the scarcity of lemmings that perchance drove it this far south.

Grasses, bowing under the strain of the stiff winds, are making circular patterns around their bases.

Icicles are hanging from the eaves, from a few inches to one that measures seven feet.

The sight of a snowy owl with watchful yellow eyes on the cold landscape may seem like an hallucination.

What if you could witness with owls' eyes the revelry of the wood mice some night, frisking about the wood like so many little kangaroos?

Still cold and blustering . . . .
How silent are the footsteps of spring!

29 January

The short January thaw has arrived, and the temperatures are reaching forty degrees. Snow is darkening and lowering. Warm air brings thoughts of spring still one and one-half months away.

I guess we have entered the time of year when winter kicks and blows to stay, and spring just pushes it until finally it leaves.

6 February

Animal tracks criss-cross the river's ice. Rabbit, squirrel and mice tracks dart from one side to the other, only stopping when they have reached the protective brush. The fox, weasel and mink tracks roam the middle, working back and forth to the edges at every likely looking clump of grass.

The screech owl has been in its nesting quarters for nearly a week.

What animal, probably hungry and cold,
made these tracks across the snow?

The brown stalks of plants (above) are all that remain of summer's richness. Foxes find hunting for prey much more difficult in winter (opposite) because the smaller prey leave their shelters only occasionally.

In winter even man is to a slight extent dormant, just as some animals are but partially awake, though not commonly classed with those that hibernate.

*The spring advances in spite
of snow and ice, and cold even.*

15 February

Snow piles shrink more each day, and the first blades of grass hurry to break through the dead brown rug of last year's memory.

The sun is climbing higher; ice is becoming combed. Puddles are forming atop the ice on rivers and lakes. The small streams then flow, cutting ever so slowly to the captive water beneath the ice.

26 February

Snow melts and settles, leaving a thin sheet of ice that if touched, triggers a chain reaction of collapse.

Leaves melt into the snow as they absorb heat from the sun, and all around the weed and tree boles are circles of melted snow.

Winter is slowly relinquishing its grip; some days make it above freezing, some only zero. This kind of weather will continue until April.

*The stream's thin ice begins to break up, and leaves
melt into the snow around the bases of trees.*

John M. Nuhn

John M. Nuhn

28 February

Small corners of the woods show signs of the coming renewal — little puddles at the cattail bases contain new duckweed; snow fleas (springtails) pop all over the snow on warmer days like animated pepper; in sheltered spots hard, ice-gripped earth turns to mud.

Spring is near, even if my hopes are snuffed out by tomorrow's predicted inch of snow. Because the snow will melt and all hopes will be realized as I anticipate summer.

A sure sign of spring: rivulets of melting snow
softly splashing down from underneath the snowpack.
Overleaf: *Twin choke cherry trees frame the sun.*

But the winter was not given to us for no purpose.
We must thaw its cold with our genialness. . . .
"Let us sing winter." What else can we sing,
and our voices be in harmony with the season?